D1030533

# A Kid's Guide to Drawing America™

# How to Draw
# Hawaii's
## Sights and Symbols

Jennifer Quasha

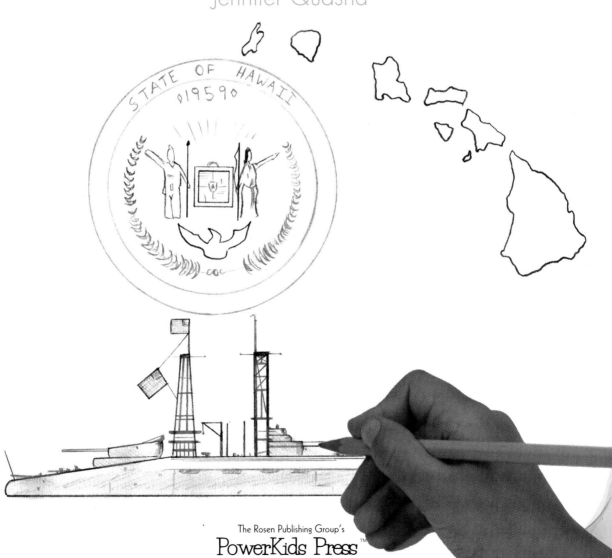

The Rosen Publishing Group's
PowerKids Press™
New York

*To Lola*

Published in 2002 by The Rosen Publishing Group, Inc.
29 East 21st Street, New York, NY 10010

First Edition

Book and Layout Design: Kim Sonsky
Project Editor: Jannell Khu

Illustration Credits: Jamie Grecco
Photo Credits: pp. 7, 16, 22 © Index Stock; p. 8 © Ray Jerome Baker, Bishop Museum; p. 9 © D. Howard Hitchcock, Bishop Museum; pp. 12, 14 © One Mile Up, Incorporated; p. 18 © Marc Muench/CORBIS; p. 20 © James L. Amos/CORBIS; p. 24 Dana Edmunds/Pacific Stock; p. 26 © CORBIS; p. 28 © Richard Cummins/CORBIS.

Quasha, Jennifer.
How to draw Hawaii's sights and symbols / Jennifer Quasha.
p.  cm. —(A kid's guide to drawing America)
Includes index.
Summary: This book describes how to draw some of Hawaii's sights and symbols, including the state's seal, the state's flag, the Dole Plantation, and others.
  ISBN 0-8239-6067-6
1.  Emblems, State—Hawaii—Juvenile literature.  2.  Hawaii in art—Juvenile literature.  3.  Drawing—Technique—Juvenile literature. [1. Emblems, State—Hawaii.  2. Hawaii.  3. Drawing—Technique] I. Title. II. Series.
  2001
  743'.8'09969—dc21

Manufactured in the United States of America

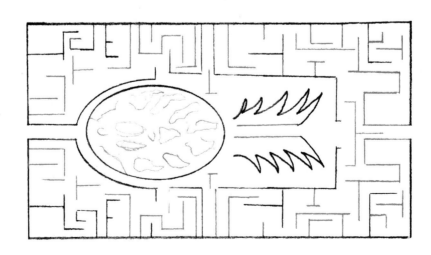

# CONTENTS

1   Let's Draw Hawaii                4
2   The Aloha State                  6
3   Hawaii Artist                    8
4   The Map of Hawaii                10
5   The State Seal                   12
6   The State Flag                   14
7   The Hibiscus                     16
8   The Kukui Tree                   18
9   The Nene                         20
10  The Lei                          22
11  The Dole Plantation              24
12  Pearl Harbor                     26
13  Hawaii's Capitol                 28
    Hawaii State Facts               30
    Glossary                         31
    Index                            32
    Web Sites                        32

# Let's Draw Hawaii

Hawaii is often called the Paradise of the Pacific. This nickname came about because of Hawaii's white beaches, colorful plants and flowers, warm climate, and friendly people. If you visit Hawaii, you will not be bored! There are plenty of things to do, such as visiting volcanoes, surfing, learning how to hula dance, or relaxing on one of the glorious beaches. A trip to Hawaii isn't complete without celebrating at a luau. A luau is a traditional Hawaiian feast that includes an entire pig roasted in an earthen oven pit, called an *imu*.

Not surprisingly, tourism is one of Hawaii's largest industries. Other industries include trade, food processing, finance, petroleum refining, and stone production industries, as well as clay and glass production industries. The sunny, tropical climate makes Hawaii a strong agricultural producer. Sugarcane, macadamia nut, pineapple, and many other plants and trees are grown throughout the islands.

Hawaii has many terrific sights and symbols. You can learn more about them and how to draw them by using this book. All you have to do is follow the step-by-step illustrations and instructions given for each drawing. A red line shows that a new step has been added. The list of drawing terms on this page introduces some of the shapes and words you'll need to know to draw Hawaii's sights and symbols. Find a quiet, well-lit space where you can draw, and get ready to have some fun!

You will need the following supplies to draw Hawaii's sights and symbols:

- A sketch pad
- An eraser
- A number 2 pencil
- A pencil sharpener

These are some of the shapes and drawing terms you need to know to draw Hawaii's sights and symbols:

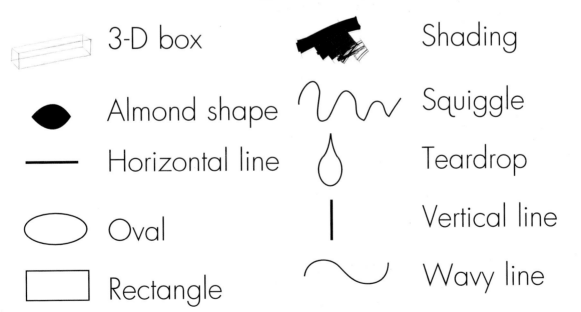

3-D box

Almond shape

Horizontal line

Oval

Rectangle

Shading

Squiggle

Teardrop

Vertical line

Wavy line

# The Aloha State

Hawaii was the last state to join the United States. It became the fiftieth state in the Union on August 21, 1959. Hawaii has a population of 1,185,500 people. The capital city is Honolulu and 423,500 people live there. Although people from Polynesia arrived in Hawaii about 1,500 years ago, less than twenty percent of the people living in Hawaii today came from these Polynesian ancestors. Today Hawaii is home to a huge range of people from many different backgrounds. In fact, Hawaii has become one of the country's most ethnically mixed states.

The highest point in Hawaii is Mauna Kea, a mountain on the Big Island of Hawaii that is 13,796 feet (4,205 m) tall. Not far away is another mountain, Mauna Loa, which is 13,678 feet (4,169 m) tall. A bit of land called Ka Lae, or South Cape, is the southernmost tip in the noncontiguous United States.

Hawaii is often called the Aloha State. Aloha means both "hello" and "good-bye" in the Hawaiian language, and also "we love you."

A Hawaiian woman wears garlands of flowers on her head and around her neck as she does the hula dance, a traditional Hawaiian dance.

# Hawaii Artist

D. Howard Hitchcock was a landscape painter, sculptor, and illustrator who was born in 1861, in Hilo, Hawaii. In 1885, Hitchcock attended the California School of Design in San Francisco for a year. When he returned to Hawaii, Hitchcock met another

This photograph, taken around 1920, shows D. Howard Hitchcock working at his easel.

Hawaiian artist, named Jules Tavernier. Jules Tavernier invited Hitchcock to join him on a trip to paint pictures of Hawaii's volcanoes. The trip had such a strong effect on Hitchcock that he decided to become a professional painter. Jules Tavernier remained Hitchcock's friend and mentor until Tavernier's death in 1889.

In 1890, Hitchcock went to study art at the Julian Academy in Paris. After three years, he returned and settled in Honolulu. Hitchcock traveled around the Hawaiian islands and painted wilderness scenes. His most famous paintings were large, 30-foot (9-m), mural-size paintings of the natural wonders of

Hawaii. Hitchcock was known for his sensitive use of light, as well as his details of Hawaii's plants and flowers. He was a pastoral painter. This means Hitchcock didn't paint Hawaii's landscapes exactly as he saw them, but in a more beautiful style based on how he felt. D. Howard Hitchcock died on New Year's Day, 1943.

*Courtesy of the Bishop Museum*

This painting, titled *View of Honolulu*, was painted using oil on canvas and measures 11" x 19" (28 cm x 48 cm). The painting is a good example of D. Howard Hitchcock's use of light and color.

# The Map of Hawaii

Niihau
Oahu
Kauai
Molokai
Maui
*Pacific Ocean*
Lanai
Kahoolawe
Hawaii

Hawaii

Map of the Continental United States

Hawaii is an archipelago in the Pacific Ocean. Although Hawaii has a total of 137 islands, there are eight main islands. These are Hawaii, Kahoolawe, Kauai, Lanai, Molokai, Niihau, Oahu, and Maui. The largest of the islands is Hawaii, also known as the Big Island. These eight islands form 6,459 square miles (16, 729 sq km) of land. Hawaii's chain of islands is 3,100 miles (4,989 km) long, but most of the small islands are less than 3 square miles (7.8 sq km) across. Hawaii's islands are actually the tips of volcanoes. Volcanoes are formed when land moves above magma, or hot spots in the earth, and releases lava. The creation and destruction of volcanoes in Hawaii has been going on for 70 million years!

1

Start by drawing Hawaii's first four islands. Notice that the biggest island is shaped like a triangle.

2

Next draw the smaller islands as shown. Notice how far away the islands are from one another.

3

| | |
|---|---|
| ☆ | Honolulu |
| 〻 | Akaka Falls |
| ○ | Dole Plantation |
| ▢ | Pearl Harbor |
| △ | Mount Kilauea |

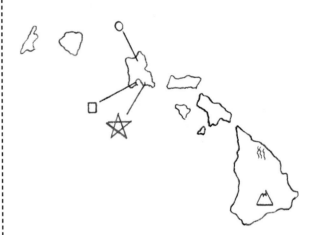

a. Draw a broken triangle to mark Mount Kilauea, Hawaii's most active volcano.
b. Use a circle to note the Dole Plantation.
c. Use a square to represent Pearl Harbor.
d. Draw a star for Hawaii's capital, Honolulu.
e. Use three wavy lines to mark the Akaka Falls.

# The State Seal

A man named Viggo Jacobson designed the state seal of Hawaii in 1895, before Hawaii became a state. The central image of the seal is a shield that is divided into four sections. On the left of the shield is King Kamehameha I. The Goddess of Liberty is on the right. The Goddess of Liberty wears a laurel wreath around her neck and a phrygian cap, and she holds the Hawaiian flag in her right hand. Below the shield is a bird called a phoenix, with its wings spread. The words "State of Hawaii" are at the top of the seal. Directly underneath these words is the year Hawaii became a state, 1959. At the bottom of the seal is the motto of Hawaii, written in Hawaiian. This motto is *Ua mau ke ea o ka aina i ka pono*, or The Life of the Land is Perpetuated in Righteousness.

**1**

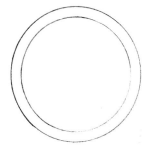

Start by drawing two large circles. Draw one circle inside the other.

**2**

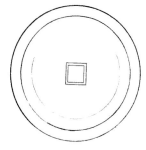

Then add a half circle and two squares.

**3**

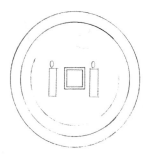

To draw the people on the seal, use two small ovals for heads and two rectangles for bodies.

**4**

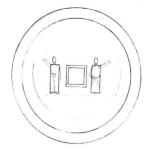

Draw in the bodies and use small rectangles for arms.

**5**

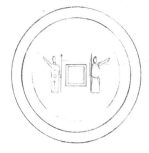

Erase extra lines and draw the spear and flag.

**6**

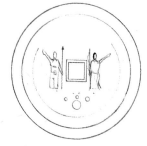

Use circles as guides to draw the main parts of the phoenix.

**7**

Fill in the outline of the phoenix and start drawing leaves around the half circle. The leaves look like upside-down *C* 's.

**8**

Erase extra lines, draw two diamonds around the "1959," and write the words "State of Hawaii."

# The State Flag

Hawaii's state flag has eight stripes that represent the eight main islands of Hawaii. At the top of the flag, the stripes alternate white, red, and blue. On the top left corner of the Hawaiian flag is a miniature flag of Great Britain. This is because, in 1794, Hawaii had close ties to Great Britain through George Vancouver. He unofficially placed the islands under British protection that year. King Kamehameha I, or Kamehameha the Great, ruled Hawaii from 1795–1819. King Kamehameha oversaw the creation of the Hawaiian flag. The flag symbolizes the various periods in Hawaii's history when the state was the Kingdom of Hawaii, the Republic of Hawaii, the Territory of Hawaii, and finally the state of Hawaii.

**1**

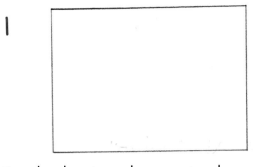

Start by drawing a large rectangle.

**2**

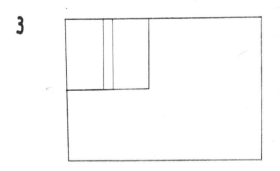

Then add a small box in the top left corner of the flag.

**3**

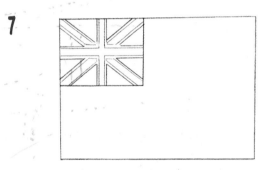

Draw a thin, vertical rectangle in the center of the small box.

**4**

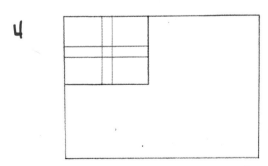

Next add a thin, horizontal rectangle to the box.

**5**

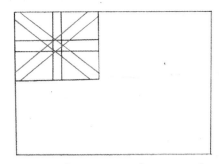

Add two more thin rectangles to make the X shape.

**6**

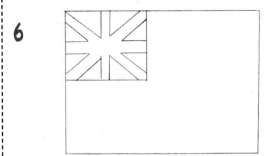

Erase extra lines and smudges.

**7**

Trace a double outline of the rectangles in the upper left-hand corner.

**8**

Add seven straight lines going sideways in the large part of the flag, and you are done.

15

# The Hibiscus

On June 6, 1988, the pale yellow hibiscus, called *pua aloalo* in Hawaiian, became the official state flower. The hibiscus has always been a popular flower in Hawaii. In fact, of all the beautiful flowers that grow there,

the red hibiscus was the favorite flower of Queen Liliuokalani, queen of Hawaii from 1891 to 1893.

Hibiscus flowers can be white, pink, red, yellow, or orange. They have shiny, green leaves. Hibiscus flowers have five petals that are from 3 to 8 inches (8–20 cm) wide. The flowers grow on plants that are from 8 to 15 feet (2.4–4.6 m) tall and from 5 to 10 feet (1.5–3 m) wide.

**1**

Start by drawing a circle for the center of the flower.

**2**

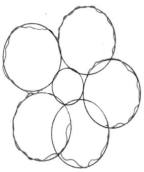

Then add five circles around the center. It's okay if they overlap.

**3**

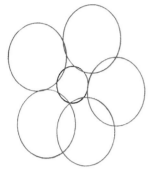

Use squiggly lines to change the five outer circles into petals.

**4**

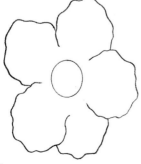

Erase extra lines.

**5**

Add five large half circles for leaves, and start to draw in the shapes.

**6**

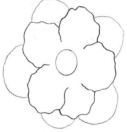

Finish drawing the shapes of the leaves.

**7**

To draw the center of the flower, use two vertical lines and a circle.

**8**

Add shading and detail to your flower. Erase any extra lines.

# The Kukui Tree

The kukui tree (*Aleurites moluccana*) was adopted as Hawaii's state tree on May 1, 1959. Kukui trees thrive in moist, tropical regions like Hawaii, Malaysia, and the Philippines. They can grow up to 90 feet (27 m) tall. They have long, pointed leaves that are grayish green in color. The kukui tree has small, white flowers with five petals. The flowers are often used to make flower wreaths and leis. The kukui tree is sometimes called the candlenut tree because early Hawaiians used kukui nuts to make oil for lighting purposes. Today oil from these nuts is used to treat dry or burned skin. People also eat the nuts and grind them up for spices, but the nuts must be roasted first. Kukui nuts that are not roasted are poisonous.

**1**

Start by drawing a small rectangle for the trunk of the tree.

**2**

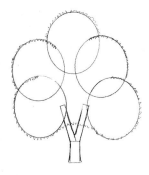

Then add two longer rectangles for branches.

**3**

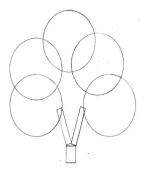

Add five circles for the shape of the tree.

**4**

Start drawing leaves around your circles. You can draw as many as you like. It helps to draw the leaves in the shape of V's.

**5**

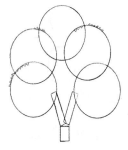

Finish your leaves and draw the shapes of the trunk and branches.

**6**

Erase extra lines, leaving behind the shape of your tree.

**7**

Add shading and detail to your tree. You can blend the pencil lines further by smudging them with your finger.

19

# The Nene

The nene, or Hawaiian goose, became the state's official bird in 1988. The nene has a long, off-white neck with black, vertical stripes. It has a black ring around the base of its neck. The feathers on its back and body are gray and brown. The nene is from 23 to 28 inches (58–71 cm) long and weighs from 4 to 5 pounds (1.8–2.3 kg). The nene is a land bird, which means it has short, small wings and less webbing between its toes than do other geese that live in the water. Hunters nearly wiped out the nene species, and by 1950 there were only about 30 nene left in the world. In 1949, the nene was protected by law. Today there are nearly 800 wild nene in Hawaii, and more than 2,000 worldwide.

**1**

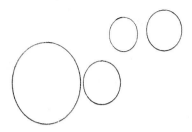

Start by drawing four circles for the bird's head, neck, and body.

**2**

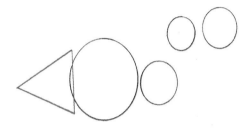

Then add a triangle for the tail.

**3**

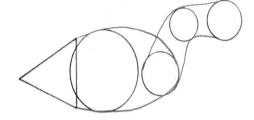

Connect the circles to form the outline of the bird.

**4**

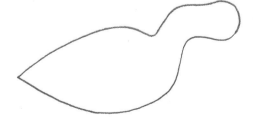

Erase any extra lines or smudges inside the bird's outline.

**5**

Draw three triangles, two for the top of the bird's legs, and one for the beak.

**6**

Then add two rectangles for the bird's legs, and two triangles for the feet.

**7**

Draw a small circle for the eye, and a rectangle for the wing.

**8**

Erase any extra lines, and add detail and shading to your bird.

# The Lei

Leis are wreaths or necklaces made from flowers, leaves, shells, and feathers. Leis are offerings of "aloha" generally given by Hawaiians to visitors and loved ones. When a person receives a lei, he or she often receives either a kiss or a hug, or both! In the 1930s, visitors whose ships docked in Hawaii were greeted by hula dancers wearing grass skirts and leis. These hula dancers offered visitors their own lei wreaths. When the visitors went back home, they spread the word about the beautiful leis and the warm greetings of the Hawaiians. It was not long before leis became a symbol of Hawaiian hospitality that was recognized around the world. Today Lei Day is held every May 1. Hawaiians celebrate Lei Day by wearing at least one lei around their necks.

**1**

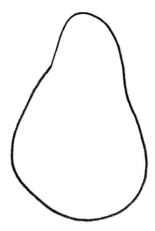

Start by drawing the shape of the necklace.

**2**

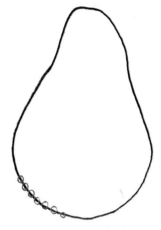

Then add small circles all the way around.

**3**

Add flower petals between the circles, using *S*-shaped, curvy lines.

**4**

Add detail in your petals. Short, straight lines will do.

**5**

Add shading to your lei, and you're done!

# The Dole Plantation

The pineapple garden maze at the Dole Plantation in Honolulu is in the *Guinness Book of World Records* as the world's longest maze. The maze covers 2 acres (.8 ha) of land. The maze's path is 1.7 miles (2.7 km) long and is made with 11,400 plants. Many of the plants are hibiscus plants, Hawaii's state flower. In the center of the maze is a garden shaped like a pineapple. The Dole Plantation was named after Jim Dole, the Pineapple King, who pioneered the pineapple industry in America. Today the plantation hosts nearly one million people a year. They come to see the maze, to learn about the pineapple and the history of Dole, and to buy these fruits. The plantation sells more than 3,500 pineapples a week!

1

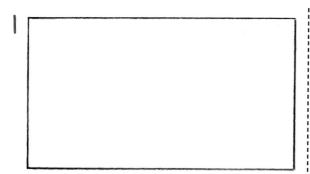

Start by drawing a large rectangle.

2

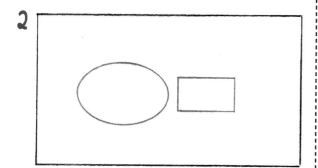

Then add an oval and a rectangle for the pineapple.

3

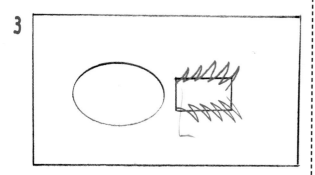

Use triangle shapes to draw the pineapple leaves.

4

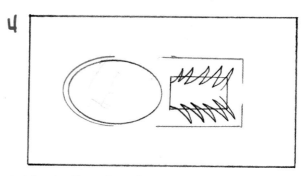

Add a half oval and a rectangle shape.

5

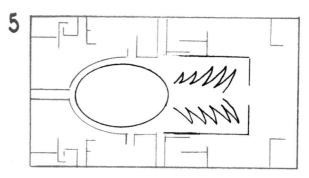

Erase extra lines. Then use a ruler to add lines for the maze. It's easier if you make the lines on top the same as the lines on the bottom.

6

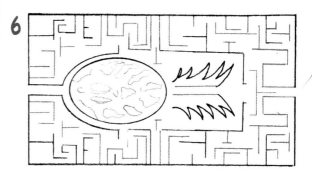

Keep adding lines until the rectangle is full.

# Pearl Harbor

   Honolulu is Hawaii's capital city. Pearl Harbor is a natural harbor 6 miles (9.7 km) northwest of downtown Honolulu. When Kamehameha I ruled the island of Hawaii from 1795 to 1819, so many pearls were found in oysters from the harbor that it was given the name Pearl Harbor. In the United States, Pearl Harbor is known as the location of the Navy Base where the USS *Arizona* and other ships were attacked by the Japanese on December 7, 1941. This caused the United States to enter World War II. Today a marble memorial, called the USS *Arizona* Memorial, stands in Pearl Harbor above the battleship's sunken wreck.

**1**

To draw the USS *Arizona*, start by drawing a long rectangle and a rounded triangle.

**2**

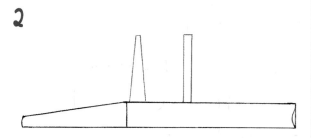

Then add a triangle and a skinny rectangle on top of the first rectangle. Draw a curved line at the rectangle's right end.

**3**

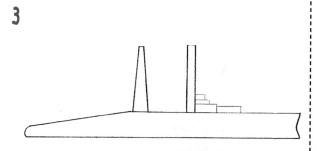

Erase extra lines and add four small, stacked rectangles.

**4**

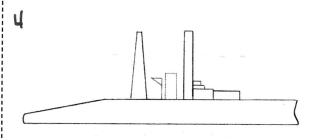

Add another upright rectangle and a tiny triangle on a stem.

**5**

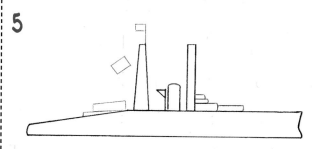

On the left side of the ship, add four more rectangles, two for the gun and two for flags. Round all the edges.

**6**

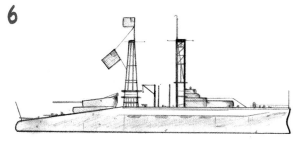

Add shading and detail to your ship. Erase any extra smudges, and you're done.

# Hawaii's Capitol

The state capitol building in Honolulu was built to look like a volcano. The building is surrounded by a reflecting pool. This is to remind people of the islands of Hawaii, which are surrounded by water. Forty pillars placed around the building represent the coconut palm trees that grow all over the Hawaiian islands. Above the large pillars, groups of eight smaller pillars support the top floor. Each set of eight pillars signifies the eight Hawaiian Islands. In front of the building is a statue of Father Damien, a Roman Catholic priest from Belgium, who helped many Hawaiians suffering from leprosy. Behind the capitol building is a statue of Queen Liliuokalani, queen of Hawaii from 1891 to 1893.

**1**

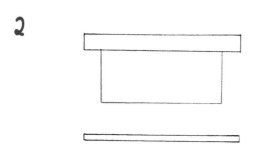

Start by drawing two long rectangles.

**2**

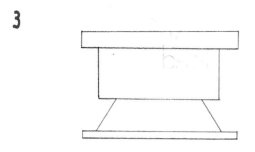

Then add a large rectangle that is attached to the top rectangle. Note the different thickness of each rectangle.

**3**

To make the base of the building, add two slanted lines.

**4**

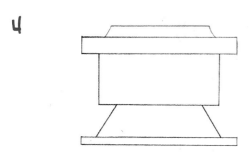

On the very top of the building, draw a rectangle with two slanted sides.

**5**

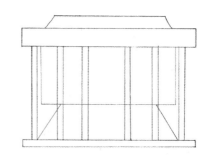

Add six long, thin rectangles for columns.

**6**

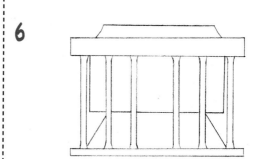

Erase extra lines and smudges, and curve the top and bottom of each column.

**7**

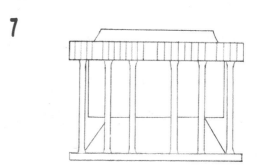

Draw thin lines in the roof of the building, as shown.

**8**

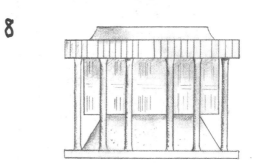

Add shading and detail to your building. Erase any extra smudges, and you're done.

29

# Hawaii State Facts

| | |
|---|---|
| Statehood | August 21, 1959, 50th state |
| Area | 6,459 square miles (16,729 sq km) |
| Population | 1,185,500 |
| Capital | Honolulu, population, 423,500 |
| Most Populated City | Honolulu |
| Industries | Tourism, trade, finance, food processing, production of stone, clay, glass products |
| Agriculture | Sugarcane, nursery stock, tropical fruit, livestock, macadamia nuts |
| Gemstone | Black coral |
| Sport | Surfing |
| Motto | The Life of the Land is Perpetuated in Righteousness |
| Nicknames | The Aloha State, The Pineapple State |
| Flower | Hibiscus |
| Bird | Nene |
| Tree | Kukui |
| Song | "Hawaii Ponoi" |
| Fish | Humuhumunukunuku apua'a |

# Glossary

**alternate** (AL-tur-nayt)  To go every other one, or taking turns.

**ancestors** (AN-ses-turz)  Relatives who lived long ago.

**archipelago** (ar-kih-PEH-luh-goh)  A group of islands.

**destruction** (dih-STRUK-shun)  Great damage or ruin.

**ethnically** (ETH-nik-uhl-lee)  Having to do with a group of people who share the same language or culture.

**hula** (HOO-luh)  A Polynesian dance using hip and hand movements.

**lava** (LAH-vuh)  A hot liquid made of melted rock that comes out of a volcano.

**leis** (LAYZ)  Necklaces of flowers.

**leprosy** (LEH-pruh-see)  A disease of the skin that causes nerve damage, paralysis, and deformity of the limbs.

**luau** (LOO-ow)  A traditional Hawaiian feast.

**magma** (MAG-mah)  A hot, liquid rock underneath Earth's surface.

**mentor** (MEHN-ter)  A trusted counselor or guide.

**mural** (MYUR-ul)  A picture painted on a wall or ceiling.

**phoenix** (FEE-nihks)  A mythical bird.

**phrygian** (FRIH-jee-en)  Of or related to Phrygia, an ancient, extinct area in Indo-Europe.

**plantation** (plan-TAY-shun)  A very large farm where crops are grown.

**Polynesia** (pah-lih-NEE-zhuh)  A country in Southeast Asia.

**sensitive** (SEN-sih-tiv)  Able to see small differences.

**thrive** (THRYV)  To be successful; to do well.

**tropical** (TRAH-pih-kul)  Of or related to a region of Earth that is near the equator. It is always warm in the tropics.

**unofficially** (un-uh-FIH-shel-ee)  Not recognized by the government.

**wreath** (REETH)  A circle of leaves and/or flowers woven together.

# Index

**C**
capital, 6, 26
capitol, 28
climate, 4

**D**
Dole, Jim, 24
Dole Plantation, 24

**H**
hula dance, 4

**I**
industries, 4

**K**
Kamehameha I (king
    of Hawaii), 12,
    14, 26
kukui tree, 18

**L**
Lei Day, 22
leis, 16, 22
Liliuokalani (queen of
    Hawaii), 16, 28
luau, 4

**M**
motto, 12
mountains, 6

**N**
nickname, 4, 6

**P**
Pearl Harbor, 26
pineapples, 24
Polynesia, 6

**S**
state bird, 20
state flag, 14
state flower, 16, 24
state seal, 12

**U**
USS *Arizona*, 26

**V**
volcano(es), 4, 10,
    28

# Web Sites

To learn more about Hawaii, check out this Web site:
www.state.hi.us